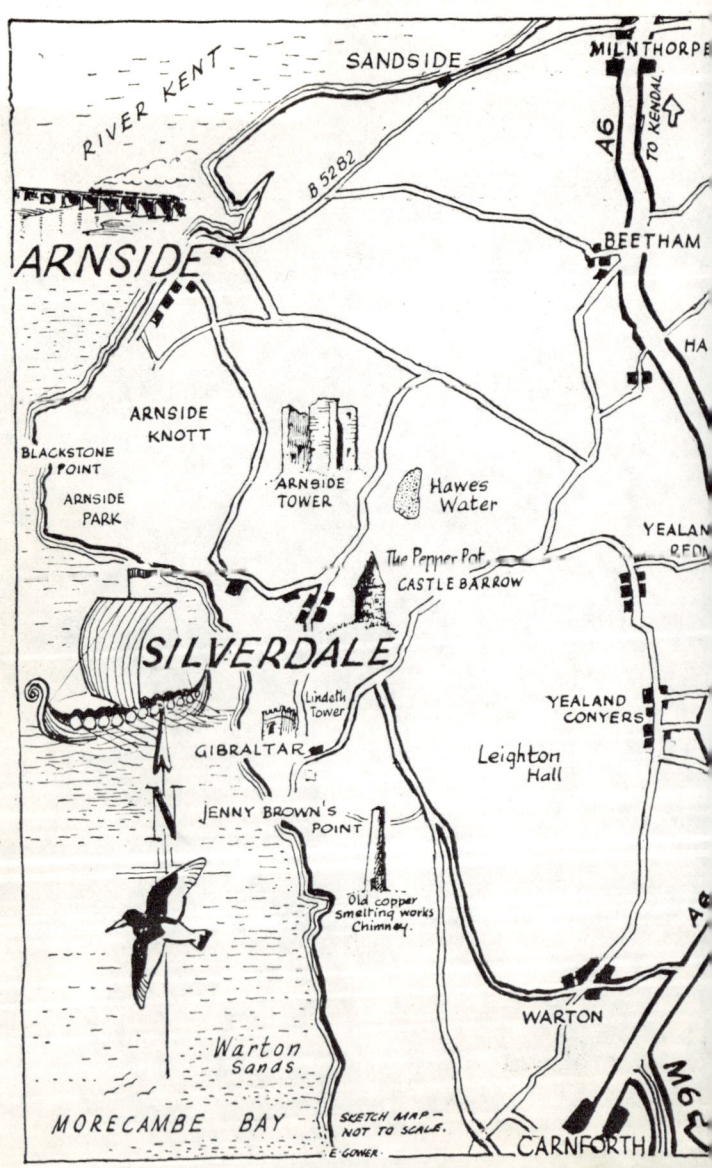

RIVER KENT

SANDSIDE

MILNTHORPE

A6

TO KENDAL

B 5282

BEETHAM

ARNSIDE

HA

ARNSIDE KNOTT

BLACKSTONE POINT

ARNSIDE TOWER

Hawes Water

ARNSIDE PARK

The Pepper Pot
CASTLE BARROW

YEALAND R'F'D'N

SILVERDALE

Lindeth Tower

YEALAND CONYERS

GIBRALTAR

Leighton Hall

JENNY BROWN'S POINT

Old copper smelting works Chimney.

A6

WARTON

M6

Warton Sands

SKETCH MAP — NOT TO SCALE.

MORECAMBE BAY

E. GOWER

CARNFORTH

Arnside and Silverdale

A Practical Guide
for Visitors

Compiled by "Cumbria"

Illustrated by J. J. Thomlinson

DALESMAN BOOKS

1976

35p.

THE DALESMAN PUBLISHING COMPANY LTD., CLAPHAM (via Lancaster), NORTH YORKSHIRE

First Published 1976

ISBN : O   85206   355   5

Printed in Great Britain by
GEO. TODD & SON,
Marlborough Street, Whitehaven

CONTENTS

Map by E. Gower

Arnside Tower

INTRODUCTION

A MOTORIST on the A6 has a swift, smooth passage between Carnforth and Milnthorpe. It is less congested than it was following a northward extension of the M6. On either side are broad green fields. Far away to the right lie some of the big rounded hills of the Pennines. Closer, to the left, are lesser heights, thickly wooded, with grey chimney smoke rising from houses at Yealand Redmayne and Yealand Conyers — villages that seem to be half smothered by trees. The Bela river is seen close to Beetham. Above the road bridge the water is clear and smooth as glass. Lower down, about the paper mill, it is white with spray where it tumbles over a shelf of rock against which the salmon hopefully fling themselves each year on their spawning runs.

Comparatively few travellers suspect that beyond the low western hills — beyond the coppice woods and the plantations — is an area of the North Country with as varied a range of attractions for holiday tourists as any part of Lancashire to which, surprisingly, the area partly belongs. Everywhere there are trees, from stately individuals in the parks of Dallam and Leighton to the dense coppice woods which once had an important commercial value (bobbins, hoops for barrels, charcoal for gunpowder, oak to be boiled and riven for agricultural baskets). The area has its high spots (Arnside Knott, the highest at 522 feet, and Castlebarrow with its curious monument known as "Pepper Box"). It has its low spots, like Leighton Moss and the marshes close to Morecambe Bay and Kent estuary.

There is the appeal of birds and animals in thoroughly natural settings. Dense flocks of waders trip across the mudflats of the shore on thin winter days. Duck settle in their hundreds on Leighton Moss, an area of reed and water which is supervised by the Royal Society for the Protection of Birds. Leighton has among its nesting birds the elusive bittern. Red deer, some of them "royals," having twelve points to their antlers, roam in the vicinity. Fallow deer

5

inhabit parkland at Dallam and Levens, light phase beasts at the former and a dark variety at the latter.

The transport revolution which began last century opened out this area as never before. Arnside and Silverdale have no canals. The waterway from Lancaster to Kendal is not far away, and the man-made watercourse crossed between Warton and Silverdale was a cut designed to take away water pumped from Leighton Moss at a time when the Moss was rich farming land. In 1857 the Furness Railway was opened, with stations at Silverdale and Arnside and (near the latter place) an imposing viaduct across the Kent estuary. This somewhat restricted the coasting trade and made it necessary for the Arnside pier to be built.

The railway encouraged businessmen to bring their families to the district. They had the assurance of good communications by rail with places like Kendal and Lancaster. Tourists used the railway, and pleasure steamers from Morecambe visited Silverdale Cove. The service stopped when the Kent channel altered its course and the area close to Silverdale rapidly silted up.

Now the majority of visitors arrive by car. They are mainly people looking for space in which they can entertain themselves. So parties of visitors trudge along the many well-marked footpaths; they play games on the marshes close to Morecambe Bay.

GENERAL INFORMATION

Early closing : Thursday.

Bus services : Ribble services 553 and 554, Lancaster to Kendal via Carnforth, Silverdale, Arnside and Milnthorpe. Service 553 via Warton and Crag Foot; service 554 via Yealand.

Rail services : Stations at Carnforth, Silverdale and Arnside served by services from Preston and Lancaster to Barrow. Carnforth also served by Leeds - Morecambe services.

Caravan sites :

O. & D. B. Barber, New Barns Farm, Arnside. Tel. Arnside 761446.

Holgates Caravan Parks Ltd., Cove Road, Silverdale. Tel. Silverdale 508.

Scout Crag Caravan Site, Silverdale Road, Warton.

Fell End Caravan Park, Slackhead Road, Hale. Tel. Milnthorpe 2122.

Silver Ridge Caravans, Silver Ridge, Hale. Tel. Milnthorpe 3198.

Beetham Caravan Park, Beetham. Tel. Milnthorpe 2552.

Banks :

Barclays (Arnside, Carnforth and Milnthorpe).

National Westminster (Arnside, Silverdale, Carnforth and Milnthorpe).

Midland (Milnthorpe).

Libraries : Lancaster Road, Carnforth; Silverdale (Branch library).

Sailing : Arnside Sailing Club.

Golf : Silverdale golf course near station.

Bowls : Bowling green near Elmslack, Silverdale.

ARNSIDE

Arnside Village : At the time of the Norman Conquest, this village was given to Ivo de Talebois. It became a part of the vast Beetham Manor. Great developments such as in church-building (Cartmel and Furness Abbeys were rising beyond the Sands) seemed to by-pass Arnside. Here the people quietly tilled land and fished in the sea. When there were threats from marauding Scots (maybe from pirates as well) people found sanctuary in Arnside Tower. It was one of a number of pele towers built around Morecambe Bay. The pele at Arnside was owned by the Harrington family. In more settled times, peles either became ruined through neglect (as at Arnside) or were incorporated into country homes (which happened at Levens).

Close to the front at Arnside is Ye Olde Fighting Cocks, an inn of 1660 which has recently reverted to its original name after being known as the Crown Hotel for many years. There was no promenade at Arnside until the 19th century. The highest tides washed right up to some of the buildings, such as Saltcotes (1679), which was built close to the estuary. Here pits were dug and lined with clay so that salt could be collected from sea water. Ecclesiastically, Beetham was the main centre. The folk of Arnside had to walk to Beetham to attend church. They used the same path when it was time for them to pay their dues. Part way to Beetham they ascended a limestone cliff by rough-hewn steps which today are known as the Fairy Steps.

Arnside was still very remote and almost unknown to outsiders in the latter part of the 18th century. The Rev. William Hutton, chronicler at Beetham (he was vicar from 1762 until 1811) wrote that it consisted of "meadows, mosses, roots of the mountain or Knott, and sand." There were only 23 houses. At this time some ambitious schemes were devised for reclaiming land from the Bay, and an embankment was constructed between the shore of Arnside Tower. The real opening-up and development of Arn-

Arnside village and foreshore

side followed the arrival of holidaymakers early in the 19th century and, midway through that century, the construction of the "Ulverstone and Lancaster Railway" (later absorbed by the Furness Railway).

Arnside promenade and the embankment were made about 1897. The old Arnside boathouse of the Crossfields was moved from central Arnside to Ashmeadow (originally an inn). Here boat-building continues though with smaller craft than those for which Crossfields became famous — the trawlers of Morecambe Bay. These trawlers have the sheer lines of yachts. They carried an enormous amount of sail until the coming of diesel engines in recent years, when modifications were necessary.

There is a strong tide at Arnside, but the estuary is safe if a boat enthusiast takes reasonable precautions. The high tide produces a bore which sweeps up from the bay and exhausts itself against the viaduct.

Arnside church celebrated its centenary in 1966. This was originally in the large parish of Beetham, and became a district chapelry in 1870. Five years later a curate-in-charge was appointed. The parish of today includes Arnside, Carr Bank and Storth, with a population of just over 2,200. Part of Carr Bank and Storth are still in the civil parish of Beetham. Arnside church is almost filled with worshippers on Sunday mornings in summer. Most of them are visitors to the village.

A well-known ornithologist who lives at Arnside doubts if there is anywhere else on the west side of England where one can record a bigger variety of bird species than within a ten mile radius of Arnside. He has seen 133 species of birds on the front at Arnside alone. In winter wild geese, mainly greylags, are found on the Meathop marshes, across the water, and in their evening roosting flight the skeins often pass right over Arnside. Avocets and spoonbills have been seen, but the more typical birds are those of the winter tideline — the vast flocks of knot and dunlin, the herds of curlew and packs of oystercatchers.

Arnside pier

Kent Viaduct : Anyone who visits Arnside today looks hard and long at the viaduct which spans the tidal Kent. It almost shouts to be noticed because of the scale of its construction. The railway lines rest on 50 piers which rise from the shifting sands of the estuary. Making a viaduct here was enough to daunt any engineer. Borings showed that there was no suitable foundation for at least 90 feet. James Brunlees, an engineer who had experience of sandy terrain in coastal Ireland, came up with the solution, which Mr. J. A. Barnes detailed in a book called "All Around Arnside" :

Mr. Brunlees hit upon the device of supporting the bridge on hollow iron piles, each with a broad iron disc at the bottom, six feet in diameter. The piles were sunk in the sand partly by working them with a circular motion as a washer-woman works her "dolly-legs," partly by forcing water down the pile under hydraulic pressure. The sand and water then boiled up inside and all around the pile, which sank by its own weight. Several lengths were jointed together until a depth of twenty or thirty feet had been reached. . . . The bridge is therefore supported like a camel in the sands of the desert by the mere breadth of its own feet.

Work on sinking the piles in the sands of Kent extended from October 1856 until July 1857. A month later the first train had passed over the viaduct. A contemporary print shows a trellis structure, and there was a single line. The structure was reinforced by brick at the beginning of the 1914-18 war, and this work took longer than the original construction. At the same time an "apron" with a thick cement top of boulders and cement was added.

The completion of a viaduct across the Kent raised problems not immediately connected with the railway. There was the matter of navigation on the estuary. Ships had long used it to reach wharves at Sandside and Milnthorpe. A visitor notices that one span of the viaduct is broader than the others. It was intended for the passage of ships, but ultimately the railway had to provide a pier at Arnside. Its stubby remains protrude from the promenade just below the line of the viaduct. The Morecambe Bay and Kent

Estuary Preservation Society (formed originally to oppose a Manchester plan to dam the estuary) raised money to purchase the pier and to place public seats and plants there for the enjoyment of visitors.

A second consequence of the viaduct was the silting up of land about it. This included 1,000 reclaimed acres which were later to be known collectively as "Brogden Marsh," after the family — father and three sons — who were the chief directors of the railway. Mr. George Edward Wilson, of Dallam Tower, owned the original foreshore to the estuary. He began a court case at Lancaster Assizes in 1867 to claim 410 acres of the new marsh. Wilson lost his claim. Aggrieved at the decision, he appealed for a new trial. This was granted but the Lancaster decision was upheld.

Arnside Knott Nature Trail : Arnside Knott is as high in feet as the railway viaduct is long in yards. The figure is 522. The Knott dominates a rocky peninsula on which the village stands. Here the first human settlement in the district would be made. Iron Age hill folk, known as the Brigantes, were possibly on Arnside Knott when the Romans came this way during one of their bold northern conquests. The name Knott is of Saxon origin and it means "rounded hill." Those who walk up the Knott, or motor part way, will see a mountain indicator. The Knott was common land until the enclosure act of 1821; today most of it is owned by the National Trust, and it is in the special care of Arnside Parish Council.

The Arnside Knott Nature Trail begins at the mountain indicator, the route being shown by numbered posts and blobs of red paint on trees and stones. The Trail encompasses larch, silver birch, juniper, beech, wych elm, oak, sycamore, self-sown ash and yew trees, as well as such features as ant hills, an erratic glacial boulder, carboniferous rock and iron deposits. A guide to the Trail, including a map, is available from the Clerk to Arnside Parish Council and local retailers.

Walks around Arnside :

1. To Fairy Steps and Beetham. Take road by the station and keep straight on to Black Dyke Farm, on left. Turn left through yard, cross railway, through fields to Hazelslack. Cross road and over stile to path which leads through a field and then climbs through woodland, to Fairy Steps, which are cut on the limestone escarpment. Path leads on through woodland to Beetham, which has a Norman church (return to Arnside via Dallam by walking to main road from Beetham church and turning left). Track on left leads to Dallam Park, where deer can be seen. Path leads over Bela river to Arnside-Milnthorpe road.

2. Shore to Silverdale. This is a pleasant walk, yet the way is rocky in places (return to Arnside via Arnside

Fairy Steps

13

Tower). Alternatively, walk along shore to a lane with a house at the corner; turn up lane, and bear right at the top (follow road and bear right at fork, signposted to New Barnes Bay, about one mile. Lily Woods are on the right). At farm take track to left, and then along track which bears right, leading to point above White Creek. Path continues round edge of cliff at Far Arnside. Eventually, way turns inland by a farm and some cottages. Here it joins the Silverdale road.

Arnside Tower Farm

THE KENT ESTUARY

THE River Kent descends a thousand feet in a course of only 25 miles. It is therefore one of the swiftest rivers in England. Kentsiders, proud of the river and at the same time a little over-awed by its depredations in times of flood, claim it to be *the* swiftest river. Few people have seen the point at which the Kent flows into the estuary close to High Foulshaw. The land round about is private property. For all its speed the Kent is of modest size up to the point where it enters the wide estuary. Quite soon it is joined by the Rivers Bela and Gilpin. The merged waters then take a course close to Dallam and Sandside.

At low tide you see the channel clearly, for the sand bars (marked Milnethorpe Sands on the maps) are high and firm. You can also make out the points at which the dykes draining the mosses northward of Kent estuary add their quota of fresh water to the estuary. When the tide sweeps in from Morecambe Bay, overwhelming the high sands and, in winter, displacing many thousands of shore birds, this Kent estuary resembles a vast lake. Arnside's railway viaduct, constructed on the line of an old ford at a point where the estuary narrows, seems to be an impenetrable barrier. Its 50 piers are set close together and, viewed from some angles, give the impression of a continuous brick wall.

The shoreline is low. Kent estuary is therefore a place for remarkable views, obtained from only a few feet above sea level. In sight are the Cumbrian mountains and part of the Pennine Range.

The major road has a brief encounter with the edge of the water at Sandside — it has been out of sight of the estuary from Arnside —and here the tarmacadam is broad enough to allow for car parking. Some cars belong to sea anglers from lower Lancashire who seek the fluke (or flounder), a distinctive flatfish of Morecambe Bay. At one time, when there was marsh close to Sandside, hundreds of cars could be parked off the road. Fickle Kent eroded away the marsh up to the railings and now hardly any greensward remains. The sea can be adventurously close. A high tide backed by a high wind sends water spilling deeply over stretches of road. People living beside the Kent recall great floodings of the Meathop and Foulshaw marshes, which lie across the estuary. They also tell when spray from the sea has been thrown right over trains using the viaduct.

Ships of all kinds have floated on the estuary. There have been fine yachts competing in Arnside regattas. The course for a yacht race was twice from Arnside pier to Holme Island and round it, which is not possible now since a causeway was built. Small coasters called at landings which are now mud or green marsh. Steamers drew up against Arnside's pier after a high tide crossing from Morecambe.

In the reign of Henry VIII when there was an increase in the number of boats using the quiet, sheltered creeks and landings of the Kent estuary — some of them operated by pirates and smugglers — an Admiral was appointed for the locality. He was one of the Clifford family, and the title was held by his descendants long after the need for an Admiral had passed. About the same time the Kent estuary had a customs officer. The first mention of such an official occurred in 1589, and there may have been a customs house at Milnthorpe. Others were built at Sandside, then Arnside, as the estuary silted up and it was necessary for boats to be tied up nearer to the open sea. The Arnside customs house was demolished in 1925 at a time of road widening. It was used for its original purpose until about 1854.

Old records inform us of six landing places along the estuary and two just outside it. Kentside landings were at Milnthorpe, Dixies, Sandside, St. John's Cross, Arnside and Blackstone Point. The other two lay at Heathwaite and Knowhill. All were on Kent's southern shore. Few remains have been found of the port of Milnthorpe. Possibly the ships entered the Bela at high tide and were grounded against staves to keep them upright while one cargo was unloaded and another taken aboard.

Milnthorpe had trade with places as far distant as Glasgow and Liverpool. Flax and farm produce were brought in from Northern Ireland. Iron for the forges was imported from Scotland. Leaving the port of Milnthorpe were leather, slate, gunpowder from the Sedgwick and Gatebeck works, hoops, limestone, the products of Milnthorpe factories and the varied manufactures of Kent. In Arnside's great days as a port, stone was shipped to Blackpool to be used in the construction of the promenade. Seaborne trade flourished at a time when inland communications were poor (local turnpikes were not constructed until well into the 19th century). Kent estuary had eight inns but only two remain — The Ship at Sandside and Ye Olde Fighting Cocks at Arnside.

Locally-grown timber went into a shipbuilding yard which flourished at Arnside as early as 1715 (a sloop was built at this time). Wild weather thinned out the local shipping fleet. The schooner *Hope* was capsized near Arnside in 1853, and the *Wild Duck,* battered by a storm when it was off Ashmeadow Point, was driven into the grounds of Ashmeadow House.

Since the days of commercial shipping, Kent estuary has silted up further, and it is rare for a boat to be seen above the railway viaduct. The estuary is a quiet area of mud and sand and water.

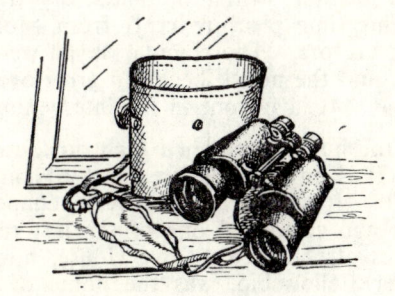

AROUND SILVERDALE

Silverdale : Silverdale's houses are spread out at the sides of a network of small roads, close to the lush green marshland at the edge of Morecambe Bay and surrounded on most other sides by coppice-type woodland. It has long been known as walking country because of the variety of scenery within a short distance. Silverdale — the modern spelling — first appeared in 1500, by which time the Tower which is named after Arnside (but is in fact closer to Silverdale) had been built. The ruins of today have a maximum height of 50 feet, but something of the old pele character remains in the immensely thick walls. It is thought to date from the late 15th century, when there was the threat of raids by Scotsmen and pirates.

In Silverdale itself the shore can be approached from a point where a line of old cottages stands (there is a free car park) and also from the Cove. Here the tall cliffs have a number of caves, two of them natural and one a mine working. Down the lane to the Cove were carted bobbin wood, grindstones and other goods to be shipped from Silverdale by boats which were mainly coasters from Greenodd. The Kent channel moved about 1850 and the area silted up. About the turn of the century, the sea was back at the Cove, following a further switch of course by the fickle Kent estuary. This time pleasure craft from Morecambe were able to land visitors. The channel stayed well inshore until about 1920, and the marsh began to grow over again about 1930. It has spread far out in the intervening years.

Look at the building perched high on the cliff area near the Cove. It is an oratory, created by Henry Boddington in the 1860s. It served as his private chapel for a time. Boddington had converted one of the last remaining crofters' cottages of the area. Cove House, now used by the Stone Bower Fellowship, was the home of the Rev. W. Carus Wilson, master at the school at Cowan Bridge which was attended by the Bronte sisters from Haworth. When there was an outbreak of low fever, Charlotte and Emily stayed at Cove House for a short time until their father, the Rev. Patrick Bronte, collected them and took them home to Haworth.

The present St. John's Anglican church was consecrated in 1886, but it succeeded an older building, dating back to the 12th century. In the following year Silverdale acquired its "Pepper Box," as a memorial erected on Castlebarrow was to be known locally. The memorial was built to commemorate the jubilee of Queen Victoria. Castlebarrow is now the property of the National Trust.

The Bay has silted up so much that it is safe to walk along the shore from Silverdale to Arnside at low tide on turf which has been close-cropped by sheep until it is almost as fine as a bowling green. Sea-washed turf from various parts of Morecambe Bay is in keen demand for just this purpose. There are muddy pools, and there are acres of sea pinks in season.

Jenny Brown's Point: A popular walk from the centre of Silverdale village ends at Jenny Brown's Point. About 1650 the house originally known as Gibredding (now Gib-

Silverdale village

19

raltar Farm) was built beside this road. "Redding" is an old term for enclosure. The tower which can be clearly seen from the road was erected about 1825 by a banker named Fleetwood. Mrs. Gaskell, biographer of Charlotte Bronte, loved to visit Gibraltar and had a special fondness for sitting on the tower to watch the sun setting over the Bay. Nearby, on the road to Hazelwood, is the Wolf Howe Gallery which shows original paintings and rural crafts.

An attraction at both Silverdale and Arnside is that the walks are well signposted and, in some cases, the references to walks on direction posts have equal prominence with those for motorists. The way to Jenny Brown's Point is a cul-de-sac for wheeled traffic, but there is limited parking space at the end. Grey Walls (on the left of the road) has a rock garden which from time to time is open to public inspection. A small charge is made and the proceeds are handed over to the Royal National Lifeboat Institution.

Where the road to the Point ends there is an old quarry. The marshes are close by. Most visitors want to know about Jenny Brown. Very little is indeed known about her.

Chimney of copper smelting works, Jenny Brown's Point

She was an old lady who kept pigs, and she occupied the large house on the shore (referred to as Brown's House on old maps) about 250 years ago. A grey chimney rising in isolation not far away served a copper smelting works which was established at the end of the 18th century. Welsh labour was used for its building. The boiler and machinery arrived by boat and were taken away by boat. The copper ore came from Crag Foot. This site has yielded copper since the days of Elizabeth I.

One final feature of interest is the toe, or weir, which protrudes into the Bay, extending seawards for about a mile, though most of it is now buried by sand. This substantially-built wall was connected with a scheme put forward in 1864 to reclaim Silverdale Sands. It was to cost £84,000. Common's approval was obtained, but there was an appeal against it and the scheme was rejected by the Lords. The man who appealed was left to foot the bill for a great part of the cost already entailed.

Walks Around Silverdale :

1. About 3½ miles. Start at the Post Office; turn left, then immediately right, following a lane through an allotment to Woodwell. Pass Woodwell and go along the bottom of a wood called Beggar's Rake to a stile at the top. Cross the road, pass through a gate, and follow a footpath to the top of the hill, where there is another stile. Go over this stile to the next stile (summit of Healds Brow) and then on to the last stile before you enter Leighton Moss bottom. Turn left, and walk to the road at the top of the village.

2. About 6 miles. From the Cove, go up Cove Lane; turn left and walk until the caravan site is reached. Cut across the Common until a path is reached on your right; turn right, and you will come to the top of a footpath at Elmslack. Walk to the bottom of Elmslack. Proceed up a path until you come to a stile leading into Eaves Wood. The wood is about half a mile long. Cross the railway to a stile almost opposite where you came out of the wood.

Walk to the top of Arnside road; carry on along the road for about 200 yards; turn right down to Haweswater Lake. Walk round the lake and carry on down a lane until you come to Station Road. Walk up Station Road for about a quarter of a mile; then take a stile on the right which brings you to the golf links. Cross the road to the stile on the opposite side. Walk down the footpath to the Dingle and Burton Well meadow bottom; cross stream by a natural bridge. Proceed up the wood (Burton Well Wood) until you come to Silverdale Common. Turn left and you have an easy walk to Silverdale Post Office.

Part of Eaves Wood is laid out as a Nature Walk; illustrated guides are available from Mrs. G. A. Turnbull, "Hawthorn Bank," Cove Road, Silverdale.

3. Short walk to the Lily Woods. Start at the Cove and walk up Cove Lane; turn left, across the common, and do not turn right. Proceed until you come to a stile, which should be crossed. In about 100 yards you come to another stile, which brings you to Arnside road. Follow a narrow lane down to Juan Well Bank. Keep up to the path side in the wood. Pass the Deserted Village on the right. You are then in the Lily Woods. Return to Silverdale by the shore.

There are numerous footpaths around the village, well signposted.

22

NORTH FROM CARNFORTH

Carnforth: The name Carnforth means "ford of the Kerne." This was the old name for Keer, a river which is only really noticed as it flows across low-tide Morecambe Bay and is negotiated with some caution by the cross-bay walkers. Early in the 18th century John Lucas jotted down details of local happenings which are of great value to anyone who seeks to piece together details of the past. In his time, Carnforth had a ship-building industry. Ships also called here before the river channel silted up.

The fortunes of Carnforth boomed with the six blast furnaces that produced pig iron. There is no heavy industry today, but Carnforth retained its importance and its large population when it became a railway junction. The main line is the Lancaster-Carlisle, opened in 1846, and two other systems are connected to it. There is the Furness railway, which passes through the Silverdale and Arnside countryside and crosses the Kent estuary by the imposing viaduct. It is a surprisingly level line, with no nasty gradients. At no point is it more than 50 feet above the level of the sea. The old Midland line, via Wennington, approaches Carnforth from the east and crosses over the main line to approach the station from the west.

The M6 carries an enormous and varied traffic to a junction with the A6 just north of the town. The motorway extends up the Lune Valley to Shap and then on to Carlisle and Scotland.

Steamtown: With some thirty preserved locomotives and five miles of track covering twenty acres, Steamtown claims to be one of the foremost live steam museums in Britain. Sited off Warton Road, Carnforth, its approaches are well-signposted and there is ample car parking space. Steamtown is open daily from 9-0 a.m. to 6-0 p.m., and locomotives are in steam on Sundays between March and October and at Bank Holidays.

The birth of Steamtown came about in 1969 when British Railways closed their engine shed at Carnforth. A group of railway enthusiasts who had purchased steam locomotives, and were looking for suitable accommodation for them, were able to take over the shed to form the nucleus of the museum. Since then the venture has gone from strength to strength, progress being greatly helped by the running of steam specials on British Railways from 1972. Locomotives from Steamtown have worked to Barrow, Sellafield (south of Whitehaven), Leeds, Carlisle and Horwich.

The locomotive stock at Steamtown changes periodically, but at the time of going to press outstanding exhibits include "Flying Scotsman"; two Great Western locomotives — "Pendennis Castle" and "Raveningham Hall"; Merchant Navy class "Canadian Pacific"; a massive French National Railways 4-6-2; and a German Federal Railways oil-fired 4-6-2.

Warton : Less than five minutes' car journey time away from Carnforth, Warton lies at the edge of a thickly wooded district, with the heights of Warton Scar immediately behind it. It has a population of 3,000. The main attraction for visitors is the church, and not just because of its architectural features. Here are still vivid, inscribed reminders of the Washington family, from which the first President of the United States sprang.

The first Washingtons lived in County Durham. There is an important town of that name in Durham today. Somewhere about 1350 a John de Washington arrived at Warton, and the family prospered. They were staunch churchfolk, and Robert Washington paid for the building of the tower in 1475. He marked his generosity by placing an inscribed stone on the outside. It had the arms of his family — two bars and three mullets, the first "stars and stripes" — which were later to figure in considerably greater number on the flag of the United States. The stone weathered badly, and when the tower was restored a few years ago it was moved inside. Each Independence Day the "Stars and Stripes" is flown from the tower. The most recent flag given to the church had been flown on the Capital building in Washington.

Visitors are naturally interested to know how George Washington, the first President, fits into the picture. He descended from a Laurence Washington, who was born in 1500. Laurence did not stay at Warton. He was at Northampton in 1530, married to Elizabeth, widow of William Gough. Laurence bought Sulgrave Manor in 1539, and it was Washington property for three generations. John Washington, great-grandfather of George Washington, emigrated to Virginia in 1656. Warton Old Rectory, now being restored, dates back to the 13th century and is one of the oldest examples of domestic buildings in the North-West.

A northward-running road leads from Warton to the Yealands — Yealand Redmayne and Conyers — which are half canopied by trees. Minor roads lead from them to the A6.

Yealand Redmayne

Leighton Hall

Leighton Hall: The fine house, the seat of the Gillow family and, today, the home of Mr. and Mrs. Reynolds, is "open to view" from the beginning of May to the end of September on Wednesdays, Sundays and Bank Holidays, 2-30 p.m.—6-0 p.m. It is most handily approached from Warton, and a cattle grid at the main entrance to the park gives easy access. The hall has a facade of gleaming white limestone and, built in the "Gothick" style of about 1800, looks almost like a piece of stage setting. This facade covered up a building in the Adam style, built on the site of an older building in 1763.

This site, close to Morecambe Bay, with a range of Lakeland mountains as a "backcloth" when the weather is clear, has long been occupied. Over 700 years ago Adam d'Avranches had a fortified manor, having received a grant of the land from William de Lancaster, Baron of Kendal, in 1173. Since then there have been 24 owners of the property. Only twice has the ownership passed by sale. Richard

Gillow, grandson of Robert Gillow (founder of the Lancaster furniture business of Gillow & Co.), bought the property from his cousin, Alexander Worswick, in 1822.

A footpath from Yealand Conyers passes through Leighton Park, skirts the edge of the Hall, and descends to Leighton and Grisedale Farms. Beyond them is a causeway across Leighton Moss, leading to a road which is not far from Silverdale railway station. Red deer wander between Grisedale Wood, Round Top Wood and on to Warton Crag. They are indigenous to the country.

Leighton Moss : Owned by the Leighton Hall estate but rented to the Royal Society for the Protection of Birds, Leighton Moss is nationally known.

The Moss was once rich farming land. An old marsh had been reclaimed in 1847, and when it was drained a pumping station was installed. The pump was operated by steam power, and the fuel — coal — could be handily carted from the station at Silverdale. Towards the end of the first world war, when coal was not easily obtained, the pump stopped and the area reverted to marsh. There are 400 acres, with 175 acres of open water and the rest mainly the common reed (phragmites) and willow scrub. The R.S.P.B. has worked hard to keep the area attractive to birds, with the clearing of areas of weeds. Channels through which water passes to the old cut have also received attention. Water from Leighton was pumped into the cut at low tide in the days before the inundation. It enters Morecambe Bay close to Jenny Brown's Point.

Motorists visiting the area usually do so from Warton, and the cut is crossed just before the railway is reached. Bear right at the junction, and right again to cross the railway bridge near Silverdale station, and Leighton Moss is seen spreading across the lowland to the right of the road. The reception centre at Myers Farm is open from 10-0 a.m. to 5-0 p.m. on visiting days, and small parties may obtain permits without prior booking. Visiting days are Wednesdays and Sundays (all year), Thursdays (April—September) and Saturdays (April—August).

Access is permitted to the main causeway, and a hide has been placed here so that casual visitors can look at birds on a stretch of water without the birds being aware of their presence. Osprey, harriers and buzzards are among the big birds which are seen fairly regularly at Leighton. The Moss is most famous for its breeding bitterns and reed warblers, as well as for such birds as shoveler, teal, garganey, water rail, grasshopper warbler, kestrel and redpoll. Muddy areas in front of the hides attract the migrant waders.

Leighton Moss

BEETHAM AND MILNTHORPE

SITED beside the river Bela on the main A6 road from Carnforth to Kendal, Beetham can provide the contrast of an ancient building (the church, with a Saxon base to the tower) and the paper-making concern of Henry Cooke & Co. Ltd. Many people have taken the trouble to explain the derivation of the name of the river. Leland passed through the village and called it "River Bythe, a pretty river, which likelyhood resort." Dr. Burn thought the name was Beetha, for one of the grants to the Priory of Conishead in the reign of Henry II used this name. The Rev. William Hutton, vicar for about half a century from 1762, commented that there are two fields on the north side either so called "from Beela side, from Belliside, old French for pretty sides, or rather, I think, from the God Bell, worshipped by the Brigantes. If so, the River was probably called Bell, and the God worshipped on the top of the hill."

On the Haverbrack or west side of the river stands Heron Mill, one of the best surviving examples of a water-driven corn mill still possessing its original machinery. Under the auspices of a Trust, it has been restored to working order and at the time of going to press was to be open to the public from 2-0 p.m. to 5-0 p.m. each day except Monday and Saturday. Robert Gambles describes the Mill in the Dalesman publication "Man in Lakeland," and comments:

"Here, by the river Bela where a mill has stood for 750 years and more, where the canons of Conishead Priory once ground their corn, there is every hope that within a short time water power will turn the great wheel again and the millstones once more receive grain from the hoppers. Then, we may recapture something of the poetry felt by Maggie in her mill on the Floss — 'the dim delicious awe as at the presence of an uncontrollable force — the meal forever pouring, pouring — the fine white powder softening all surfaces and making the very spidernets look like a fairy lacework — the sweet pure scent of the meal . . .'."

Beetham village and church

Just across the way is the modern paper mill. Its history began in the way of many country mills, with the grinding of corn. In 1788 the premises were converted for the production of paper.

Beetham's church is one of the most ancient — and beautiful — buildings in Westmorland. Six bells dangle in its old grey tower, which rests on stonework that was put in place in Saxon days. There is Norman work on the south side, and Early English to the north. The tomb of Sir Thomas de Beetham and his wife is topped by effigies in stone. These were badly mutilated by Richard Sill, of Whasset, a feoffee of Beetham School, "who headed a mob and obliged the master and the scholars with some drunken Soldiers of Cromwell, or rather Fairfax, to brake the painted Glass Windows and abuse the Inside of the Church." Visitors to Beetham remember the approaches to the Church long after they have forgotten the inscriptions on the memorials and tombs. Trellises enclose one of the long paths, and over them rambler roses are trained. This

30

unusual and picturesque decoration was first arranged to commemorate the wedding of George V and Queen Mary in 1892.

Beetham stands in gentle country, and the land round about is stony and light. Mixed farming is carried on, including dairying, feeding and sheep. Corn, oats, wheat and turnips are grown, and the land also supports lowland breeds of sheep and cattle. Across the low country to the east lies Farleton Knott. P. J. Mannex visited this grey fell when he was compiling his *History of Westmorland,* which was published in 1849. He discovered seven springs on the summit "with several musical stones possessing, it is said, all the richness of the pianoforte. The tone is best produced by striking gently upon the stones with six wooden mallets, and the music may be executed by three performers, one playing the melody, another an inner part, and the third the fundamental bass."

* * * * *

THE best approach to Milnthorpe is from Arnside and the Kent estuary. The main beauty is at the point where the road crosses the Bela and, away to the right, can be seen the lovely parkland of Dallam, where a herd of fallow deer has been long established. The deer do not often venture close to the Bela in the hours when most visitors are about, but they can usually be seen by those who follow the footpath through the park. This route passes close to Dallam Tower, a stately home belonging to the Wilson family from its completion in 1720 until recent times. There are wild duck and swans on the Bela, and those who walk across a footbridge at the end of the village will usually discover that scores of ducks swim close by seeking scraps of food.

Milnthorpe is a large village with an astonishing variety of employment, which helps to maintain a population of 1,600 people (an increase of about 600 people during the past 30 years). Men and women find work in paper and comb mills and at a modern milk factory. There is a prospering quarry. Several large garages exist for heavy lorries and local employers include haulage firms, builders' merchants and the Forestry Commission. You might describe Milnthorpe as a village with its sleeves rolled up. Some of the children leaving Milnthorpe School go to Heversham Grammar School, which has celebrated the 350th anniversary of its founding by Edward Wilson of Nether Levens. Some older people find homely accommodation at Tattersall's almshouses, originally built in 1884 through the generosity of William Tattersall. Milnthorpe has ample car parking in the attractive market square on the east side of the A6.

Milnthorpe parish was cut from the old parish af Heversham and therefore its church is not very old. The building was opened in 1837 (it had cost about £1,200). The milk factory, close to the main railway line, is operated by Messrs. Libby. Here evaporated milk is prepared, but work has also extended into milk products as well. The milk reaching Libby's factory comes from farms ranging from the Lyth Valley northwards, and from parts of Yorkshire and Lancashire in the south.

Beetham village